A Pocket Guide to

Core Web Vitals

Andy Stubbs

invisibleloop
Pocket Books

invisibleloop.com

For Jane, Oscar and Harry

Contents

Chapter 1

About

User experience can make or break your website in today's fast-paced digital landscape. Enter Core Web Vitals: Google's definitive standard for web performance. "A Pocket Guide to Core Web Vitals" is your comprehensive guide to understanding and optimising these critical metrics for tomorrow's web.

This book is meticulously designed to provide a step-by-step approach to mastering Core Web Vitals. Whether you're a beginner looking to get your feet wet in web performance or an experienced developer striving for that perfect score, this book is for you.

What You'll Learn:

- **Fundamentals of Web Performance**: Navigate the intricate world of web performance metrics and understand why Core Web Vitals are a game-changer.

- **Deep Dive into LCP, FID, and CLS**: Master the three pillars of Core Web Vitals—Largest Contentful Paint, First Input Delay, and Cumulative Layout Shift. Learn to measure, analyse, and improve these vital signs of a healthy website.

- **Tools and Techniques**: Get hands-on with the tools that help you monitor Core Web Vitals, including Google's Web Vitals Extension, Lighthouse, and Chrome DevTools.

- **Real-World Case Studies**: Benefit from in-depth case studies that demonstrate successful optimisation strategies in action.

- **SEO and Beyond**: Discover the impact of Core Web Vitals on search engine rankings and learn best practices to stay ahead of the game.

By the end of this book, you will not only be equipped to optimise your own website but also to make informed decisions that enhance user experience, improve SEO rankings, and ultimately, drive success.

About the Author

Andy, a seasoned software engineer, boasts an illustrious career spanning over 24 years in web and mobile development. A testament to perseverance and passion, much of his expertise is self-acquired. Driven by an innate desire to share and educate, Andy has an expansive portfolio encompassing websites, mobile applications, desktop software, and command-line scripts crafted to enhance productivity. Through every line of code and keystroke, he embodies the essence of continuous learning and the joy of sharing knowledge.

Chapter 2

Introduction

Why Core Web Vitals Matter

In an era where our lives are increasingly intertwined with digital experiences, the performance of a website isn't just a technical concern—it's a critical component of user engagement
and satisfaction. Core Web Vitals, developed by Google, serve
as the primary metrics for measuring this quality of user experience. However, they're just the tip of the iceberg. Other crucial
metrics like Total Blocking Time (TBT) and Time to First Byte
(TTFB) also play a vital role in comprehending and improving
web performance.

Who Should Read This Book

Whether you're an aspiring web developer, a seasoned professional, or a business owner aiming to enhance your web presence, this pocket guide aims to be your indispensable companion. Understanding Core Web Vitals, as well as auxiliary metrics like TBT and TTFB, is no longer optional; it's a necessity for anyone who wishes to succeed in today's competitive digital landscape.

Structure of the Book

This book is structured to offer a logical progression into the world of Core Web Vitals and additional web performance metrics:

- **Part One** provides an overview of web performance metrics, setting the stage for the in-depth exploration of Core Web Vitals and supplementary metrics like TBT and TTFB.

- **Part Two** dives deep into the Core Web Vitals: Largest Contentful Paint (LCP), First Input Delay (FID), and Cumulative Layout Shift (CLS). You'll also find dedicated sections on TBT and TTFB, helping you gain a rounded view of web performance.

- **Part Three** offers hands-on guidance for using various tools to measure and monitor these metrics.

- **Part Four** shares real-world case studies, common pitfalls, and practical advice based on real-world experiences.

Through clear explanations, practical examples, and actionable insights, "A Pocket Guide to Core Web Vitals" aims to empower you to create websites that aren't just functional but also delightful to use.

So, let's embark on this journey towards a faster, more efficient, and user-friendly web. Your users will thank you, and so will your business.

Chapter 3

Overview of Web Performance

What is Web Performance?

Web Performance is the measure of how quickly and smoothly a website or web application loads, interacts, and responds to user inputs. It encompasses a range of metrics, such as page load time, responsiveness, and visual stability, all of which contribute to the overall user experience. In simple terms, web performance answers the question: "How well does this website work for the end-user?"

Evolution of Performance Metrics

Over the years, performance metrics have evolved to become more nuanced and user-centric, reflecting the growing complexity and capabilities of web technologies. In the early days of the web, rudimentary metrics such as "Page Load Time" were often considered adequate for assessing a website's performance. Yet, as web applications became increasingly intricate and laden with features, these simple measurements became insufficient.

The web community responded by developing a more diversified set of performance indicators. We've transitioned from basic metrics like "Time to First Byte" (TTFB), which primarily focuses on server response time, to more sophisticated ones such as "First Contentful Paint" (FCP) and "Time to Interactive" (TTI). These newer metrics provide a more comprehensive view of the user experience, capturing not only how quickly a page loads but also how smoothly it interacts with the user.

Today, Core Web Vitals—Largest Contentful Paint (LCP), First Input Delay (FID), and Cumulative Layout Shift (CLS)—are at the forefront of this evolution. These metrics are specifically designed to provide tangible targets for developers, helping them optimise the aspects of performance that most directly impact the user experience. Far from being mere technical jargon, they are integral in shaping the modern web, enabling developers to build websites that are not only fast but also intuitive and user-friendly.

Importance of User Experience

Figure 3.1: Photo by Elisa Ventur on Unsplash

User experience is no longer just a buzzword; it's a cornerstone for online success. A well-performing website encourages user engagement, lowers bounce rates, and can even improve SEO rankings. Core Web Vitals are Google's way of emphasizing that user experience should be at the forefront of web development practices. By optimising these metrics, you are directly contributing to a more pleasant and engaging user experience, which can have a domino effect on your website's success, from visitor retention to conversions.

Chapter 4

What Are Core Web Vitals?

Definition and Objectives

Core Web Vitals are a set of metrics introduced by Google to quantify aspects of a website's user experience. Specifically, these vitals measure the speed, responsiveness, and visual stability of a web page. The objective behind Core Web Vitals is to offer a standardised set of metrics that focus on user-centric outcomes, ultimately encouraging web developers to build websites that offer a superior user experience.

The Three Pillars: LCP, FID, and CLS

Core Web Vitals comprise three primary metrics, often referred to as the "Three Pillars":

1. **Largest Contentful Paint (LCP)**: This metric measures the time it takes for the largest content element (usually an image or text block) to be fully displayed on the screen. An optimal LCP provides the user with a sense that the page is loading quickly.

2. **First Input Delay (FID)**: FID gauges the time between a user's first interaction with a web page (e.g., clicking a link or tapping a button) and the browser's response to that interaction. A low FID is crucial for a website to feel responsive.

3. **Cumulative Layout Shift (CLS)**: This metric quantifies the amount of unexpected layout shift in the visual content of a webpage. A low CLS score ensures that page elements don't jump around, providing a more stable and pleasant browsing experience.

By mastering these three pillars, web developers can significantly improve the performance and user-friendliness of their websites, thereby meeting the objectives that Core Web Vitals aim to achieve.

Chapter 5

Largest Contentful Paint (LCP)

What is LCP?

Largest Contentful Paint (LCP) is a performance metric that quantifies the time it takes for the largest content element—be it an image, video, or text block—to be fully rendered on the screen. Unlike other load metrics that might focus on elements like DOM readiness, LCP aims to gauge how quickly a user perceives that a web page is 'useable.' A faster LCP often correlates with a more positive user experience.

Understanding LCP Scores

Figure 5.1: LCP example from the Chrome Core Web Vitals browser extension

LCP scores are usually measured in seconds, and they can generally be categorised into three groups:

1. **Good**: An LCP score of 2.5 seconds or less is generally considered good and indicates that the webpage is delivering a fast experience.

2. **Needs Improvement**: LCP scores between 2.5 and 4 seconds signal that the page could be optimised for better performance.

3. **Poor**: An LCP score of over 4 seconds is poor and suggests that the page's performance is likely to be causing a negative user experience.

It's essential to aim for a 'Good' LCP score to ensure that you're providing a satisfactory user experience and potentially bene-fiting from SEO advantages.

Measuring LCP

To accurately measure LCP, you can utilise a variety of tools and methods. Here are some of the most popular:

1. **Chrome DevTools**: Open Chrome's developer tools, navigate to the 'Performance' tab, and record a page load. LCP will be marked in the timings section.

2. **Google PageSpeed Insights**: This web-based tool provides an array of performance metrics, including LCP, along with recommendations for improvement.

3. **Web Vitals Chrome Extension**: This browser extension displays Core Web Vitals, including LCP, in real-time as you browse the web.

4. **Google Search Console**: If you have your website ver-ified, you can check the 'Core Web Vitals' report to see aggregated LCP data for your site.

Improving LCP

Improving your LCP score is a multi-faceted endeavour that often involves:

1. **Optimising Images**: Compress images and use modern file formats like WebP for better performance.

2. **Lazy Loading**: Implement lazy loading for off-screen images and media, so they only load when needed.

3. **Server Response Times**: Opt for faster hosting, and consider implementing a Content Delivery Network (CDN) to improve server response times.

4. **Code Splitting**: Split your JavaScript and CSS into smaller chunks, so that only necessary code is loaded initially.

5. **Preloading Critical Assets**: Use the `rel=preload` attribute to preload essential resources that contribute to LCP.

By taking targeted action to address these areas, you can improve your LCP score, thereby enhancing the overall user experience on your website.

Chapter 6

First Input Delay (FID)

What is FID?

First Input Delay (FID) measures the time from when a user first interacts with your page (e.g., clicks a button, taps a link, etc.) to the time when the browser is able to begin processing that interaction. This delay is an important user experience metric as it directly affects how interactive and responsive your website feels to the user.

Measuring FID

To measure FID, you can use tools like Google's Web Vitals Extension, PageSpeed Insights, and the Core Web Vitals report in Google Search Console. These tools help you collect real-world FID data for analysis.

Scoring FID

First Input Delay   8.600ms   99%   0 1

Figure 6.1: FID example from the Chrome Core Web Vitals browser extension

The FID scores are typically categorised into three bands, according to Google's guidelines:

1. **Good**: An FID of less than 100 milliseconds is considered good. This means that the page is highly interactive and responsive to user input.

2. **Needs Improvement**: An FID between 100 and 300 milliseconds needs improvement. The user might experience some delay, but it's not severe enough to be highly problematic.

3. **Poor**: An FID above 300 milliseconds is considered poor and could affect the user experience significantly. Delays of this magnitude usually make a page feel sluggish and unresponsive.

Understanding these scores is crucial as they directly impact the user's perception of your website's performance and responsiveness. A poor FID score can lead to frustrating user experiences and could negatively affect your site's search engine rankings.

Improving FID

To improve FID, you can:

1. **Minimise JavaScript Execution Time**: Break up long tasks to prevent blocking the main thread.

2. **Optimise Your Code**: Remove unnecessary libraries and polyfills to make your code leaner and faster.

3. **Prioritise Critical Loading**: Use the `rel="preload"` attribute to load critical resources first.

4. **Use a Web Worker**: Offload some JavaScript operations to a background thread by using a web worker.

By implementing these practices, you'll be better positioned to offer a faster and more interactive user experience, thereby improving your FID score.

Chapter 7

Cumulative Layout Shift (CLS)

What is CLS?

Cumulative Layout Shift (CLS) is a Core Web Vitals metric that quantifies the amount of unexpected layout movement on a web page. In simpler terms, it measures how much page elements jump around while a web page is loading or even after it appears to have fully loaded. A low CLS score is desirable, as it offers a more stable, user-friendly browsing experience. A high CLS, on the other hand, can lead to accidental clicks, disorientation, and a generally frustrating user experience.

Scoring CLS

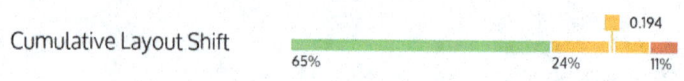

Figure 7.1: CLS example from the Chrome Core Web Vitals browser extension

The CLS score is a unitless measure, usually ranging from 0 to greater than 1. The scores are categorised as follows:

1. **Good**: A CLS score below 0.1 is considered good. This means that the page layout is stable and users are unlikely to experience disruptive shifts.

2. **Needs Improvement**: A CLS score between 0.1 and 0.25 needs improvement. Although the layout is relatively stable, users might still encounter some disruptive layout shifts.

3. **Poor**: A CLS score above 0.25 is considered poor. Users will likely experience significant layout shifts, leading to a frustrating browsing experience.

Understanding these numbers is critical as a poor CLS score can cause users to become frustrated and disengaged, potentially affecting conversion rates and search engine rankings.

Measuring CLS

Measuring CLS can be accomplished through several tools, each offering different levels of detail and insight:

1. **Chrome DevTools**: Accessible via the 'Performance' tab, it provides a timeline where layout shifts are indicated, along with a total CLS score.

2. **Google PageSpeed Insights**: This tool provides a comprehensive analysis of web performance, including CLS, and offers suggestions for improvement.

3. **Web Vitals Chrome Extension**: Useful for real-time tracking, this extension displays Core Web Vitals, such as CLS, as you browse.

4. **Google Search Console**: In the 'Core Web Vitals' report, aggregated CLS data for your website can be viewed, helping you identify problematic pages.

Improving CLS

Improving your CLS score primarily involves stabilising the layout of your web page. Here are some effective strategies:

1. **Specify Dimensions**: Always define dimensions for images, iframes, and other media elements. This prevents them from causing unexpected layout shifts as they load.

2. **Avoid Inserting Content Above Existing Content**: Unless it's in response to a user interaction, don't insert new content above existing content, particularly if it pushes other content down.

3. **Use Placeholders or Skeleton Screens**: For dynamic content or lazy-loaded elements, using placeholders can keep your layout stable until the actual content is loaded.

4. **Optimise Font Loading**: Utilise `font-display: optional` or `font-display: swap` to prevent text from causing layout shifts as fonts load.

5. **Minimise Animations**: If you must use animations, ensure they're smooth and don't cause other elements to move unexpectedly.

By taking these measures, you can significantly improve your CLS score and provide a more stable, enjoyable user experience for your website visitors.

Chapter 8

FCP: First Contentful Paint

What is FCP?

First Contentful Paint (FCP) is a performance metric that measures the time it takes for the first piece of content to appear on the screen when a user navigates to a web page. Content could be anything from simple text to an image or a video element. FCP is a critical indicator of perceived load speed, as it provides an initial cue to the user that the webpage is loading and becoming interactive.

Scoring FCP

First Contentful Paint

Figure 8.1: FCP example from the Chrome Core Web Vitals browser extension

FCP is measured in milliseconds and can be categorised into three main brackets:

1. **Good**: An FCP of under 1,000 milliseconds (1 second) is generally considered to be good. This signals that the page is offering a snappy user experience.

2. **Needs Improvement**: An FCP between 1,000 and 3,000 milliseconds (1-3 seconds) may be perceived as slow, leading to reduced user engagement and possibly higher bounce rates.

3. **Poor**: An FCP above 3,000 milliseconds (3 seconds) is considered poor and is likely to significantly impact the user experience negatively.

Measuring FCP

Several tools can be used to accurately measure FCP:

1. **Chrome DevTools**: Under the 'Performance' tab, you can record a session and identify the FCP metric on the timeline.

2. **Google PageSpeed Insights**: This tool provides an overview of your website's performance, including FCP, and offers recommendations for improvement.

3. **Google Lighthouse**: Accessible via Chrome DevTools, Lighthouse offers a detailed report that includes FCP among other performance metrics.

4. **WebPageTest.org**: This online service provides granular details about various performance metrics, including FCP.

Improving FCP

Here are some strategies to improve FCP:

1. **Optimise Critical Rendering Path**: Remove or defer non-essential JavaScript and CSS that block rendering.

2. **Server Response Time**: Opt for a faster hosting service and consider using a Content Delivery Network (CDN) for quicker asset delivery.

3. **Optimise Images**: Use image formats like WebP and employ compression techniques without sacrificing quality.

4. **Use Browser Caching**: Store frequently used assets in the browser cache to expedite subsequent page loads.

5. **Preload Important Resources**: Use the `rel="preload"` attribute to give priority to crucial resources that contribute to FCP.

By focusing on these areas, you can not only improve your FCP score but also significantly enhance the user experience on your website.

Chapter 9

Introduction to TBT and TTFB

Why TBT and TTFB Matter

While Core Web Vitals—LCP, FID, and CLS—capture critical aspects of user experience, there are other performance metrics that provide valuable insights into how a website behaves. Two such metrics are Total Blocking Time (TBT) and Time to First Byte (TTFB). These metrics offer an in-depth look into server performance and main thread activity, respectively, and are essential for understanding the complete performance picture.

TBT: A Measure of Responsiveness

TBT, or Total Blocking Time, focuses on the main thread activity. It quantifies the total duration that the main thread is blocked, impacting user interactions. While TBT isn't a Core Web Vital, it's crucial for diagnosing issues related to a website's responsiveness and can be an excellent complementary metric to First Input Delay (FID).

TTFB: Server Performance Under the Microscope

TTFB, or Time to First Byte, serves as a gauge for server performance. It measures the time taken for the first byte of data to be received after a client, such as a web browser, requests a web page. TTFB can often be a culprit in slow page loads and offers actionable insights into potential server bottlenecks.

Navigating the Chapters Ahead

The following chapters will provide an in-depth discussion on TBT and TTFB, covering their definitions, methods for measurement, and tips for improvement. Whether you're a developer looking to optimise a website or a business stakeholder aiming to improve user experience, understanding TBT and TTFB will give you a more rounded view of web performance.

Chapter 10

TTFB: Time to First Byte

What is TTFB?

Time to First Byte (TTFB) is a metric used to measure the responsiveness of a web server. It's the time it takes from the
moment a user's browser requests a page until the first byte
of that page is received. Although TTFB is not part of the Core
Web Vitals, it is a crucial factor for understanding server performance and contributes to the user's perception of a fast-
loading site.

Scoring TTFB

Time to First Byte

0.232s
95%   4 1

Figure 10.1: TTFB example from the Chrome Core Web Vitals browser extension

The TTFB scores are generally measured in milliseconds and are categorised as follows:

1. **Good**: A TTFB under 200 milliseconds is considered good, indicating a responsive server that can serve the first byte quickly. Users will perceive the website as fast and responsive.

2. **Needs Improvement**: A TTFB between 200 and 500 milliseconds needs improvement. While not terrible, it indicates some latency, which could be due to server or network issues.

3. **Poor**: A TTFB over 500 milliseconds is considered poor. This long delay can frustrate users and contribute to a

negative user experience, potentially affecting search engine rankings and conversion rates.

Understanding these timings is crucial for diagnosing slow website performance and making the necessary improvements.

Measuring TTFB

Measuring TTFB involves capturing the time it takes for a client's HTTP request to receive the first byte of data from the server. You can easily view this information using browser-based tools like Chrome DevTools, server monitoring tools like New Relic, or online services like WebPageTest.org.

Here are the steps for measuring TTFB in Chrome DevTools:

1. Open Chrome DevTools (F12 or right-click > Inspect).
2. Navigate to the 'Network' tab.
3. Reload the webpage.
4. Click on the primary document request.
5. Check the 'Timing' tab for the TTFB value.

Improving TTFB

Improving TTFB can involve a mix of server-side and client-side optimisations. Here are some strategies:

1. **Server Optimisation**: Use a Content Delivery Network (CDN) to serve assets closer to the user, optimise server-side code, and consider using server caching.

2. **Database Efficiency**: Ensure your database queries are optimised. Slow queries can significantly impact TTFB.

3. **Compression**: Use GZIP or Brotli to compress server responses.

4. **Load Balancing**: Distribute incoming network or application traffic across multiple servers to ensure no single server is overwhelmed.

5. **HTTP/2 or HTTP/3**: Using the latest HTTP protocols can improve TTFB as they introduce several optimisations over HTTP/1.x.

By understanding and improving your TTFB scores, you can enhance the responsiveness and user experience of your website.

Chapter 11

TBT: Total Blocking Time

What is TBT?

Total Blocking Time (TBT) is a performance metric that quanti-fies the total amount of time when the main thread is blocked, preventing users from interacting with your website. It mea-sures the time between First Contentful Paint (FCP) and Time to Interactive (TTI), capturing how a user would experience in-teracting with a page. While TBT is not part of the Core Web Vitals, it offers valuable insights into the responsiveness of a site, contributing to the overall user experience.

Scoring TBT

TBT is measured in milliseconds and can be categorised as follows:

1. **Good**: A TBT under 200 milliseconds is considered excellent, providing a smooth user experience with minimal input delay.

2. **Needs Improvement**: A TBT between 200 and 500 milliseconds requires attention. Users might experience slight delays during interactions, affecting their perception of the site's responsiveness.

3. **Poor**: A TBT over 500 milliseconds is considered poor. Delays of this magnitude can lead to a frustrating user experience and are likely to affect engagement and conversion rates adversely.

Understanding these timings can aid in identifying bottlenecks and making improvements for a more responsive website.

Measuring TBT

TBT can be measured using various tools designed for web performance auditing, such as Google's Lighthouse and Chrome DevTools. It helps identify tasks that run on the main thread for a long time, thus causing input delays.

To measure TBT in Lighthouse:

1. Open Chrome DevTools (F12 or right-click > Inspect).
2. Navigate to the 'Lighthouse' tab.
3. Click on 'Generate report'.
4. Review the 'Performance' section to find the TBT metric.

Improving TBT

Improving TBT often involves optimising the main thread's workload to reduce long tasks. Here are some strategies for lowering TBT:

1. **Code Splitting**: Use code splitting techniques to break down large JavaScript bundles.

2. **Lazy Loading**: Defer the loading of off-screen images and other resources until they're needed.

3. **Optimise CSS**: Eliminate render-blocking CSS and inline critical CSS.

4. **Asynchronous Operations**: Use Web Workers for tasks that can run in the background without affecting the main thread.

5. **Server-side Rendering (SSR)**: This can be particularly useful for JavaScript-heavy sites to reduce the amount of client-side code that needs to be parsed and executed.

6. **Prioritise Resource Loading**: Use `<link rel="preload">` for crucial assets to ensure they are loaded as early as possible.

By understanding and improving your TBT scores, you can offer a more responsive and engaging user experience.

I hope these additions help complete your guide on web performance metrics.

Chapter 12

Core Web Vitals and SEO

The Connection

The importance of Core Web Vitals goes beyond mere user experience; they also play a significant role in Search Engine Optimisation (SEO). Since May 2021, Google has incorporated Core Web Vitals as part of its ranking algorithm. This inclusion signifies that web pages delivering better user experiences, as measured by LCP, FID, and CLS, are more likely to rank higher in search results.

The reason behind this is straightforward: Google aims to deliver the most relevant and user-friendly results. As these metrics are indicative of the quality of user experience, it makes sense for them to be part of the SEO equation. Neglecting Core Web Vitals could result in lower rankings, reduced visibility, and ultimately, less organic traffic.

Best Practices

Improving Core Web Vitals for the sake of SEO involves adhering to best practices that overlap with general web performance optimisation. Here are some key strategies:

1. **Continuous Monitoring**: Use tools like Google Search Console to monitor your site's performance regularly. Timely identification of issues can prevent SEO setbacks.

2. **Mobile Optimisation**: As mobile-first indexing is the norm, ensure that Core Web Vitals are optimised for mobile devices as well as desktops.

3. **Page Experience Signals**: Besides Core Web Vitals, consider other page experience signals like mobile-friendliness, HTTPS, and intrusive interstitials, as they also impact SEO.

4. **Competitive Analysis**: Regularly check how your competitors perform in terms of Core Web Vitals and aim to outperform them for a potential edge in rankings.

5. **Content Relevance**: While focusing on Core Web Vitals, don't forget the fundamental SEO principle—relevant, high-quality content. Even the best-performing page can suffer in rankings if the content isn't up to par.

By integrating these best practices into your web development and SEO strategy, you can improve both user experience and search engine rankings, creating a virtuous cycle that benefits your site in the long run.

Chapter 13

Tools for Measuring Core Web Vitals

Google's Web Vitals Extension

The Web Vitals Extension is a Chrome plugin provided by Google, designed to offer real-time feedback on Core Web Vitals as you browse the web. This extension is particularly useful for quick checks, allowing developers to rapidly gauge the performance of any page, including those in development or staging environments. The tool displays metrics like LCP, FID, and CLS directly in the browser toolbar, offering instant insights.

Metrics	Local metrics compared to desktop field data

Largest Contentful Paint — 2.379s — 90% — 5 5

Cumulative Layout Shift — 0.194 — 65% — 24% — 11%

First Input Delay — Waiting for input... — 94% — 3 3

Interaction to Next Paint — Waiting for input... — 73% — 17% — 10%

First Contentful Paint — 2.405s — 92% — 5 3

Time to First Byte — 0.263s — 95% — 3 2

● Core Web Vital metric   ● Pending Core Web Vital metric   ⚗ Experimental metric

Figure 13.1: Example from the Chrome Core Web Vitals browser extension

The Core Web Vitals extension can be installed via the Google Chrome Web Store.

How to Use the Web Vitals Extension

To get started, simply:

1. Install the extension from the Google Chrome Web Store.
2. Once installed, browse to the web page you'd like to evaluate.
3. Click on the Web Vitals icon in your toolbar to view the real-time Core Web Vitals metrics.

Lighthouse

Lighthouse is an open-source, automated auditing tool that provides a comprehensive performance review of your web pages. It can be run directly in Chrome, through the command line, or as a Node module. In addition to Core Web Vitals, Lighthouse evaluates other performance, accessibility, and SEO aspects, producing a detailed report with actionable recommendations. It's a robust tool suitable for in-depth analysis and ongoing performance tracking.

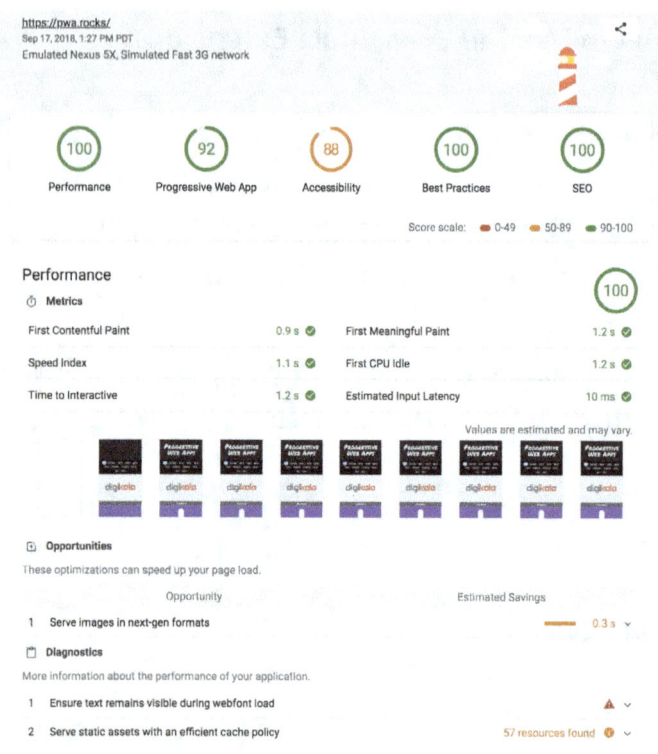

Figure 13.2: Example from the Chrome dev tools Lighthouse performance measuring tool

How to Use Lighthouse

1. Open Chrome DevTools (F12 or right-click > Inspect).

2. Navigate to the 'Lighthouse' tab.
3. Choose the categories you'd like to evaluate (Performance, Accessibility, etc.)
4. Click on 'Generate report'.
5. Review the report for insights and actionable recommendations.

Chrome DevTools

Certainly, here's a more detailed version of the text about Chrome DevTools:

Chrome DevTools is not just a set of tools; it's essentially a full-fledged development environment built directly into the Google Chrome browser. It has become an indispensable asset for modern web developers due to its extensive suite of features. This environment allows for a multitude of operations ranging from real-time inspection of HTML and CSS elements, debugging JavaScript, tracing reflows and repaints, to even conducting network performance analysis.

One of the most powerful aspects of Chrome DevTools is its 'Performance' tab. It offers an incredibly detailed timeline view, a feature that can feel like you have a microscope aimed at your web page's performance. This timeline lays out a myriad of metrics and activities as they happen in real-time, giving you insights into the millisecond-level behaviour of your website. Among these metrics, you'll find key performance indicators like Largest Contentful Paint (LCP), First Input Delay (FID), and Cumulative Layout Shift (CLS), which are part of Google's Core Web Vitals initiative.

What sets the 'Performance' tab apart is its capability for fine-grained analysis. It doesn't just highlight what's wrong; it helps you understand the 'why' and the 'how' of issues. You can drill down into each activity on the timeline to view stack traces, examine JavaScript functions causing delays, and even see a filmstrip of your web page rendering. This makes it remarkably easier to pinpoint bottlenecks and performance hiccups, providing a guided pathway to implement targeted optimisations and enhance user experience.

By integrating the ability to directly manipulate the DOM and CSS, Chrome DevTools rounds out its offerings, ensuring that developers have an all-encompassing toolkit for web development and debugging at their fingertips. Thus, with its wide range of utilities and in-depth analytics, Chrome DevTools not only helps you identify issues but also equips you with the knowledge and insights to resolve them effectively.

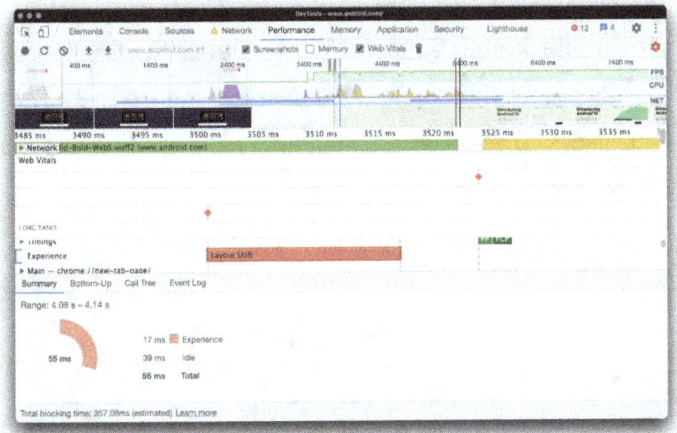

How to Use Chrome DevTools

1. Open Chrome DevTools (F12 or right-click > Inspect).
2. Navigate to the 'Performance' tab.
3. Click the 'Reload' icon to start recording performance data for the current page.
4. Review the timeline and metrics to identify areas for improvement.

Other Useful Tools

1. **Google Search Console**: This tool offers a Core Web Vitals report that aggregates user experience metrics for visitors to your website, helping you identify areas that need improvement.

2. **PageSpeed Insights**: Another Google offering, it combines data from Lighthouse and real-world usage to provide a comprehensive view of a page's performance.

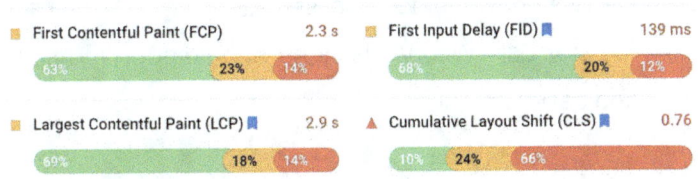

3. **WebPageTest**: This is a third-party tool that allows for advanced performance testing, including capturing videos of user journeys and comparing performance metrics.

4. **GTmetrix**: This tool provides a complete suite of performance indicators, including Core Web Vitals, and offers suggestions for improvement.

5. **New Relic**: Aimed at larger enterprises, this tool offers in-depth performance monitoring, including user-centric metrics like Core Web Vitals, within the broader context of business analytics.

6. **SpeedCurve**: SpeedCurve is a premium performance monitoring service that provides real user monitoring (RUM) and synthetic monitoring. SpeedCurve focuses on the user experience, offering insights into how various front-end factors affect a website's performance and

user engagement. It's a robust tool that integrates well with your development process, allowing you to test and monitor Core Web Vitals along with other performance and design metrics.

By understanding the strengths and limitations of these tools, you can choose the best combination to measure, analyse, and optimise Core Web Vitals effectively.

Chapter 14

Understanding and Using CrUX Tools

The Chrome User Experience Report (CrUX) serves as an invaluable resource for understanding how users interact with websites across the internet, offering a rich dataset culled from real-world browsing conditions. Compiled using data aggregated from users who have opted-in to sync their Chrome browsing history, CrUX equips developers, site owners, and stakeholders with reliable metrics about web page performance and user experience. The CrUX data can be accessed through several channels, but CrUX on BigQuery and CrUX API stand out as the two most popular and versatile tools for retrieving this valuable information.

In the following sections, we will not only discuss the distinct features and advantages that each of these powerful tools offers but will also provide comprehensive tutorials to guide you on how to effectively utilise them for your specific needs. Whether you're interested in running complex SQL queries to derive granular insights, or you prefer to fetch simplified but actionable data through a RESTful API, we'll equip you with the knowledge you need to make the most of the CrUX offerings.

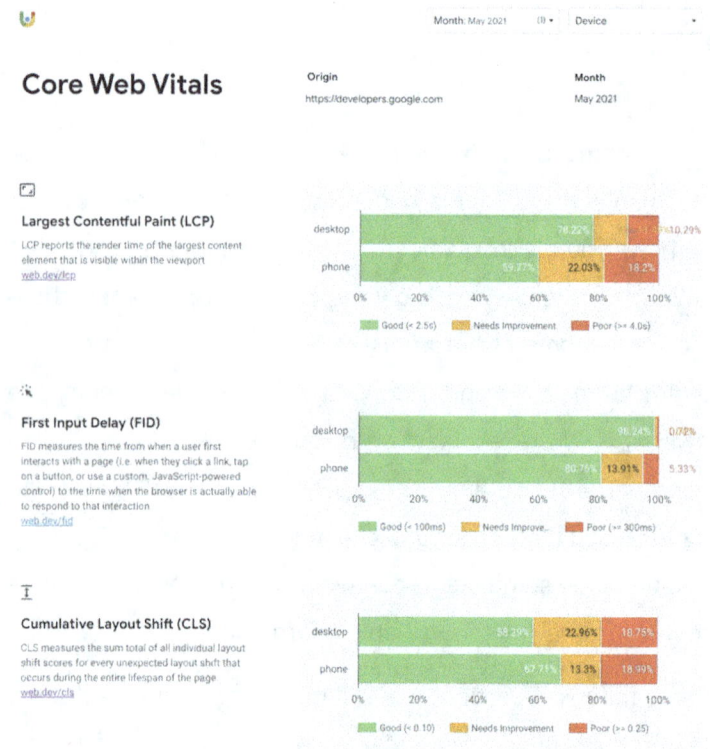

CrUX on BigQuery

What is CrUX on BigQuery?

CrUX on BigQuery is a publicly accessible dataset hosted on Google BigQuery, a fully-managed and serverless data warehouse. It allows you to perform in-depth analysis by running SQL queries on CrUX data, which includes metrics like Largest Contentful Paint (LCP), First Input Delay (FID), and Cumulative Layout Shift (CLS).

How to Use CrUX on BigQuery

1. **Access Google BigQuery**: Make sure you have a Google Cloud Platform account and navigate to the BigQuery Console.

2. **Locate the CrUX Public Dataset**: Inside the Big-Query Console, you can locate the CrUX dataset under "bigquery-public-data.chrome_ux_report".

3. **Run SQL Queries**: If you are comfortable with SQL, write queries to fetch specific data that interests you. For instance, you could query the performance of your website

for users in the UK, on mobile devices, over the past six months.

4. **Analyse and Visualise**: Once you have the data, you can visualise it using tools like Google Data Studio or directly within BigQuery.

CrUX API

What is CrUX API?

The CrUX API is a developer-friendly approach to accessing the Chrome User Experience Report. Unlike BigQuery, which requires SQL proficiency, the CrUX API provides a RESTful interface to fetch data, making it easier to integrate into existing systems and dashboards.

How to Use CrUX API

1. **API Key**: To begin with, you'll need to acquire an API key from the Google Cloud Console.

2. **API Endpoint**: Utilise the API endpoint for fetching the Core Web Vitals data for a specific website or URL.

3. **Fetch Data**: Use HTTP methods to request data. For example, you could use Python's `requests` library to pull data.

4. **Parse and Use**: The returned JSON can be parsed using your programming language of choice, allowing you to integrate this data into your applications or dashboards.

Both CrUX on BigQuery and CrUX API offer valuable insights into user experience metrics, tailored to different skill sets and needs. By understanding these tools and how to use them, you can more effectively measure, analyse, and improve your website's performance.

Chapter 15

Performance Budgets

A performance budget serves as a guideline or set of standards focused on maintaining the speed and user-friendliness of a website as it evolves. Essentially, it's a framework that helps teams make informed decisions about adding new features, content, or any elements that could potentially impact site performance. The idea is to allocate a "budget" for various types of assets or activities that affect loading time, interaction speed, and other performance metrics, including Core Web Vitals.

Why Are Performance Budgets Important?

In the web development cycle, new features, images, scripts, and styles are continually added to a website. While these elements may add value, they also consume resources and potentially slow down the site. A performance budget acts as a preventive measure, helping you consider the performance implications of each new addition. It is especially crucial for optimising Largest Contentful Paint (LCP), First Input Delay (FID), and Cumulative Layout Shift (CLS), which are part of the Core Web Vitals suite of metrics.

Types of Performance Budgets

1. Resource-based

This approach sets a limit on the size of particular resources, like images, JavaScript, and CSS files. For example, you might set a budget of 100KB for JavaScript files.

2. Milestone-based

These budgets focus on user-centric milestones, such as time to first paint or time to interactive. For instance, you could set a budget to keep the FID below 100ms.

3. Rule-based

This type employs best practices or specific performance rules, like deferring non-critical CSS or leveraging browser caching. While these don't have a quantifiable budget, they guide development practices to maintain performance.

How to Set Up a Performance Budget

1. **Baseline Assessment**: Before setting a budget, understand the current performance of your site. Tools like Lighthouse and PageSpeed Insights can be useful here.

2. **Identify Targets**: Decide which metrics are most relevant to your users. This could be based on user surveys, analytics, or Core Web Vitals scores.

3. **Quantify**: Allocate specific numerical limits to the metrics you've chosen, considering both desktop and mobile environments.

4. **Monitor and Enforce**: Make sure to integrate the performance budget into your development process. Many CI/CD tools can help enforce your budgets automatically.

5. **Review and Adjust**: As the website evolves or as new performance data becomes available, make necessary adjustments to your budgets.

Conclusion

Performance budgets act as both a guideline and a guardrail in the development process. By understanding your limits and adhering to them, you make performance an ongoing part of the conversation, ultimately leading to a better, faster user experience.

Chapter 16

Server-Side Optimisations

While a significant portion of web performance optimisation focuses on client-side improvements, server-side optimisations hold equal weight in ensuring a performant and efficient website.   Understanding and employing various server-side techniques can drastically reduce load times, improve scalability, and have a positive impact on Core Web Vitals.

Introduction to Server-Side Optimisations

Server-side optimisations involve tweaking and improving the processes that occur on the web server where your website resides. From minimising database queries to employing efficient caching strategies, these optimisations aim to speed up how quickly resources are generated and delivered to the client. This chapter will delve into key areas where you can improve server-side performance.

Web Server Configuration

One of the first places to look for performance gains is your web server configuration. Simple adjustments can lead to significant improvements:

- **Compression**: Enable Gzip or Brotli compression to reduce the size of your CSS, HTML, and JavaScript files.
- **HTTP/2**: Adopt HTTP/2 to allow for multiplexing, thus loading multiple files simultaneously.
- **Security**: Implement HTTPS for a secure and optimised connection, beneficial for both SEO and user trust.

Database Optimisations

Database performance can be a bottleneck in web applications. Employ the following strategies to improve efficiency:

- **Query Optimisation**: Use well-designed, efficient queries to reduce database load time.
- **Indexing**: Proper indexing can make data retrieval significantly faster.
- **Caching**: Store the results of frequent queries in a cache to reduce redundant work.

Caching Strategies

Caching is a powerful technique to improve both speed and reliability:

- **Object Caching**: Store database query results and reuse them to reduce database load.
- **Full-page Caching**: Store fully-rendered HTML pages to serve them more quickly to subsequent users.
- **Content Delivery Network (CDN)**: Distribute assets across multiple servers to bring them closer to end-users.

Load Balancing

As your website grows, distributing the traffic across multiple servers can help manage increased load:

- **Round-robin**: Distribute incoming requests equally across all servers in the pool.
- **Least Connections**: Direct new incoming requests to the server with the fewest active connections.

Optimising Core Web Vitals

Server-side optimisations can positively influence Core Web Vitals:

- **LCP**: Faster server response times and caching can accelerate Largest Contentful Paint.
- **FID**: Efficient JavaScript rendering and server-side rendering can improve First Input Delay.
- **CLS**: Streamlined asset delivery can prevent layout shifts, thus improving Cumulative Layout Shift.

Server Monitoring Tools

Regularly monitoring your server's performance will help you identify bottlenecks. Tools like New Relic and Grafana provide real-time monitoring capabilities and can integrate with various web servers and databases.

Conclusion

Server-side optimisations are crucial for delivering a fast and efficient user experience. The techniques and strategies discussed in this chapter should serve as a foundational guideline for your optimisation efforts. Implementing these can lead to a more robust, scalable, and performant website, which will, in turn, positively impact your Core Web Vitals.

Chapter 17

Third-Party Scripts and Advertising

Integrating third-party scripts and advertising can offer powerful functionality and monetisation opportunities for a website. However, these additions often come at the cost of performance and can negatively impact Core Web Vitals. Understanding how to manage and optimise these third-party resources is critical for maintaining a high-quality user experience.

Understanding the Impact of Third-Party Scripts

Before you add any third-party script to your website, it's crucial to understand its performance implications. These scripts

89

can introduce additional HTTP requests, increase CPU usage, and delay the rendering of important page elements.

Types of Third-Party Scripts

Here is a rundown of common types of third-party scripts you might integrate:

- **Analytics Tools**: Google Analytics, Adobe Analytics, etc.
- **Social Media Plugins**: Facebook Like buttons, Twitter feeds, etc.
- **Advertising Networks**: Google Adsense, Media.net, etc.

How Third-Party Scripts Affect Core Web Vitals

1. **LCP (Largest Contentful Paint)**: Heavy third-party scripts can delay the loading of main content.
2. **FID (First Input Delay)**: Scripts that block the main thread can make the page unresponsive to user input.
3. **CLS (Cumulative Layout Shift)**: Advertisements that load asynchronously can cause layout shifts.

Optimising Third-Party Scripts

Here are some strategies to mitigate the performance impact:

- **Async and Defer**: Use the `async` and `defer` attributes to ensure non-essential scripts don't block rendering.
- **Load Timeouts**: Implement a timeout for third-party scripts to prevent them from slowing down the entire page.
- **Conditional Loading**: Load scripts only when they are needed, and perhaps only for specific user segments.

Advertising-Specific Considerations

Advertisements can be particularly challenging due to their dynamic nature. Here are some optimisation strategies:

- **Lazy Loading**: Use lazy loading for ad placements below the fold.
- **Ad Size**: Specify ad dimensions to prevent layout shifts.
- **Quality of Ads**: Ensure that the ads themselves are optimised and lightweight.

Monitoring Third-Party Performance

Continuously monitor the impact of third-party scripts and ads:

- **WebPageTest**: Use WebPageTest to isolate the impact of each third-party script.
- **Google Lighthouse**: Run Lighthouse tests focusing on third-party performance.
- **Real User Monitoring (RUM)**: Track how real users experience your site with third-party scripts.

Conclusion

Third-party scripts and advertising offer valuable features but come with performance costs. By applying the optimisation techniques discussed in this chapter, you can strike a balance between functionality and performance, thereby positively impacting your Core Web Vitals.

Chapter 18

Building Your Own Tools for Core Web Vitals and Performance Monitoring

---

Introduction

Monitoring website performance has never been more important. With Google's Core Web Vitals serving as key performance indicators, developers need accurate, real-time metrics. Although several tools can help you monitor CWV, building your own can offer more flexibility and integration within your existing processes. This guide will walk you through creating your own monitoring tools using Google's open-source code and command-line utilities.

Using Google's Lighthouse Node Module

Lighthouse is an open-source, automated tool for auditing web pages on performance, accessibility, and more. Lighthouse offers a Node.js module that can be integrated into your own custom solution.

How to Set It Up

1. Install Node.js and npm on your system if not already installed.
2. Install Lighthouse Node module:

```
npm install -g lighthouse
```

3. You can now use Lighthouse programmatically. For example:

```
const lighthouse = require('lighthouse');
    const chromeLauncher = require('chrome-launcher');

    async function launchChromeAndRunLighthouse(url, opts,
config = null) {
      const chrome = await
chromeLauncher.launch({chromeFlags: opts.chromeFlags});
      opts.port = chrome.port;
      const results = await lighthouse(url, opts, config);
      await chrome.kill();
      return results.lhr;
    }

    const opts = {
      chromeFlags: ['--headless'],
    };

    // Use Lighthouse to audit 'https://example.com'
    launchChromeAndRunLighthouse('https://example.com',
opts).then(results => {
      console.log(results);
    });
```

Measuring Core Web Vitals Using Command Line

You can measure Core Web Vitals using various command-line
tools. These can be integrated into your CI/CD pipeline for
ongoing monitoring.

Web Vitals CLI

1. Install the package globally:

```
npm install -g web-vitals
```

2. Use the CLI to measure web vitals:

```
web-vitals https://example.com
```

Lighthouse CI

Lighthouse CI is a set of commands that make continuously running, asserting, and saving reports easy.

1. Install Lighthouse CI CLI:

```
npm install -g @lhci/cli
```

2. Run Lighthouse against a set of URLs:

```
lhci collect --url https://example.com --url
https://example.com/another-page
```

3. Assert the performance score meets your criteria:

```
lhci assert --assertions 'categories:performance>=0.9'
```

4. Save the results:

```
lhci upload
```

Conclusion

Building your own tools gives you complete control over the performance monitoring process. By leveraging Google's robust, open-source solutions and command-line utilities, you can create a tailored system that fits seamlessly into your existing workflows.

With the knowledge you've gained from this guide, you'll be well-equipped to measure, analyse, and optimise Core Web Vitals for your website.

Chapter 19

Case Studies

Real-World Scenarios

In this section, we delve into real-world case studies that demonstrate the tangible impact of Core Web Vitals on various types of digital platforms. These examples span a wide range of industries, from e-commerce websites like QuickBuy to respected news portals such as BBC News, and well-known social media platforms like Twitter. We explore how these sites initially encountered challenges related to poor Core Web Vitals scores and the measures they took to improve their performance.

QuickBuy®

1. **E-commerce Site "QuickBuy"**: Suffered from a high CLS score due to dynamically loaded product images. This resulted in users accidentally clicking on the wrong items, impacting the site's usability.

2. **News Portal "BBC News"**: Encountered sluggish LCP times due to the heavy use of advertisements and rich media elements, leading to decreased user engagement and session duration.

3. **Social Media Platform "Twitter"**: Faced FID issues because of extensive JavaScript execution, which in turn affected the user's ability to interact smoothly with tweets, likes, and comments.

Solutions and Results

For each case, we provide an in-depth analysis of the solutions that were implemen ted to tackle the Core Web Vitals issues, along with the subsequent results.

1. **QuickBuy**:

    - **Solution**: They implemented responsive image loading and defined dimensions for all visual elements.
    - **Result**: Their CLS score improved by 30%, which led to a significant reduction in accidental clicks and a 15% increase in conversions.

2. **BBC News**:

    - **Solution**: Employed lazy loading for off-screen advertisements and optimised the sizes of media files to improve loading speeds.
    - **Result**: Their LCP times decreased by 2 seconds, culminating in a 10% boost in overall page views.

3. **Twitter**:

    - **Solution**: Undertook code splitting and introduced asynchronous loading of JavaScript to reduce the burden on the browser.
    - **Result**: FID was reduced by 50 milliseconds, translating into a 20% increase in user interactions like likes and retweets.

By thoroughly examining these real-world scenarios, we gain invaluable insights into the efficacy of different performance optimisation techniques. These case studies serve not only as insightful lessons but also as practical guides, providing actionable steps that can be applied to improve your own website's Core Web Vitals. In doing so, you can enhance both user experience and SEO rankings.

Chapter 20

Core Web Vitals and Mobile Web

Importance on Mobile

In today's digital landscape, the significance of mobile web performance cannot be overstated. With mobile devices accounting for an increasing share of global web traffic, focusing on mobile-specific Core Web Vitals is crucial. Google's mobile-first indexing strategy further underscores this, making it essential for websites to optimise Core Web Vitals for mobile users.

Figure 20.1: Photo by Firmbee.com on Unsplash

Poor performance on mobile can not only lead to decreased user engagement but also adversely affect search engine rankings.

Special Considerations

When it comes to mobile devices, there are several special considerations to bear in mind while working on Core Web Vitals optimisation:

1. **Limited Resources**: Mobile devices generally have less computing power and memory compared to desktops. Optimising code for performance becomes even more crucial.

2. **Network Latency**: Mobile devices are often subject to varying network conditions, making it important to optimise for slower connections.

3. **Viewport Size**: Mobile screens are smaller, and this needs to be considered when addressing layout shifts (CLS) and visual loading (LCP).

4. **Touch Interactions**: Mobile web primarily relies on touch-based interactions, which make First Input Delay (FID) a particularly important metric to focus on.

5. **Progressive Web Apps (PWAs)**: These offer a native-app-like experience on the web and have their own set of performance considerations. Core Web Vitals should be measured and optimised for PWAs too.

6. **Localisation**: Mobile users may be globally distributed, making it important to consider geographical latency and local user experience norms when optimising Core Web Vitals.

By giving due attention to these special considerations, you can effectively optimise Core Web Vitals for mobile web, thereby ensuring a robust user experience across all types of devices and networks.

Chapter 21

Advanced Topics

Web Vitals and Progressive Web Apps (PWAs)

Progressive Web Apps (PWAs) have revolutionised the way we experience the web on mobile devices, offering features like offline access and native app-like behaviour. However, the performance considerations for PWAs can differ from traditional websites.

1. **Service Workers**: These can significantly impact FID as they control network requests, cache assets, and enable offline functionality. Ensuring that service workers are optimised is crucial for a good First Input Delay score.

2. **App Shell Model**: PWAs often employ the app shell model for quicker load times. This should be optimised to improve the Largest Contentful Paint (LCP) metric.

3. **Client-Side Rendering**: PWAs may rely heavily on client-side rendering, making JavaScript optimisation vital for both FID and LCP.

4. **Offline Metrics**: Since PWAs can function offline, it's worth considering how Core Web Vitals metrics behave under these conditions and making necessary optimisations.

Core Web Vitals in JavaScript Frameworks

JavaScript frameworks like React, Angular, and Vue have become ubiquitous in modern web development. These frameworks have their own sets of best practices and potential pitfalls when it comes to Core Web Vitals.

1. **Server-Side Rendering (SSR)**: In frameworks like Next.js (React) or Nuxt.js (Vue), SSR can significantly improve LCP by reducing the amount of client-side rendering.

2. **Lazy Loading**: Frameworks often provide native solutions or community packages for lazy loading components, which can positively impact LCP and CLS.

3. **State Management**: The way state is managed can impact FID. For instance, asynchronous state updates can help improve this metric.

4. **Virtual DOM**: While the virtual DOM can offer performance benefits, if mismanaged, it can also lead to layout shifts, affecting the CLS metric.

5. **Built-in Profilers**: Most modern frameworks come with built-in performance profilers that can assist in identifying bottlenecks relevant to Core Web Vitals.

By exploring these advanced topics, developers can gain a nuanced understanding of how to optimise Core Web Vitals in a variety of complex and modern web development scenarios.

Chapter 22

Common Pitfalls and How to Avoid Them

Frequent Mistakes

Core Web Vitals may seem straightforward, but there are several common pitfalls that developers often fall into. Recognising these mistakes is the first step toward avoiding them.

1. **Ignoring Mobile**: Many developers focus solely on desktop performance, forgetting that mobile devices often have different constraints and user behaviours.

2. **Overlooking Images**: Failing to optimise images can severely impact LCP, especially on image-heavy websites.

3. **Blocking Scripts**: Scripts that block rendering can drastically affect both FID and LCP.

4. **Inefficient CSS and JS**: Poorly optimised CSS and JavaScript files can contribute to longer loading times and layout shifts.

5. **Ignoring User Experience**: Core Web Vitals are fundamentally user-centric metrics. Neglecting the broader user experience can result in subpar performance.

Proven Strategies

To avoid these pitfalls, here are some proven strategies that can serve as practical solutions:

1. **Responsive Design**: Adopt a mobile-first approach and ensure that your website is fully responsive to different screen sizes.

2. **Image Optimisation**: Use modern image formats like WebP and apply lazy loading to offscreen images.

3. **Asynchronous Loading**: Use the `async` or `defer` attributes for scripts that are not critical to initial rendering.

4. **Code Splitting**: Break up large JavaScript bundles to make the page more digestible, thereby improving FID and LCP.

5. **CSS Optimisation**: Minify CSS and use media queries to load only the styles that are necessary for the current device.

6. **Performance Budgeting**: Set performance budgets for key metrics and ensure that any changes to the codebase do not exceed these limits.

7. **Regular Audits**: Utilise tools like Lighthouse and Chrome DevTools to conduct regular performance audits and address any emerging issues promptly.

8. **User Testing**: Finally, nothing replaces actual user feedback. Conduct usability tests to understand how real users interact with your website and use those insights to make data-driven optimisations.

Chapter 23

Preparing for Future Updates

Keeping Up to Date

The web is an ever-evolving landscape, and so are the metrics and best practices surrounding Core Web Vitals. Google periodically updates its algorithms and introduces new performance metrics, making it crucial for developers to stay updated.

1. **Follow Google's Webmaster Blog**: This is often the first place where updates are announced.

2. **Subscribe to Newsletters**: Several organisations and thought leaders in web performance offer newsletters

that keep you informed about updates and best practices.

3. **Join Online Communities**: Platforms like GitHub, Stack Overflow, and various web development forums are great for staying abreast of new trends and updates.

4. **Participate in Webinars and Conferences**: These can provide deep dives into the latest changes and are an excellent opportunity for learning and networking.

5. **Automate Audits**: Use automated tools to regularly check your website's performance metrics so you can quickly adapt to any changes in Core Web Vitals.

Resources for Continued Learning

Staying up-to-date requires ongoing learning. Here are some resources to keep your knowledge fresh:

1. **Google's Web.dev**: This site offers tutorials and guides directly from Google, providing the most accurate and current information.

2. **MDN Web Docs**: A reliable and comprehensive resource for web technologies, including performance metrics.

3. **Online Courses**: Platforms like Coursera, Udemy, and Pluralsight offer courses on web performance, often up-dated to include the latest information.

4. **Technical Books and Papers**: Keep an eye out for new publications that offer insights into web performance and Core Web Vitals.

5. **Podcasts and Blogs**: Many experts in the field host pod-casts or write blogs that are rich in both foundational and cutting-edge information.

6. **GitHub Repos**: Open-source projects can be a goldmine of information, showcasing real-world applications and techniques for improving Core Web Vitals.

7. **Social Media**: Following key influencers and organisa-tions on platforms like Twitter can provide quick updates and valuable insights.

By leveraging these resources and strategies, you can prepare yourself and your projects for future updates in the world of Core Web Vitals and web performance at large.

Chapter 24

Frequently Asked Questions (FAQs)

What Are Core Web Vitals?

Core Web Vitals are a set of user-centric metrics that quantify key aspects of web usability such as load time, interactivity, and the stability of content as it loads. They include Largest Contentful Paint (LCP), First Input Delay (FID), and Cumulative Layout Shift (CLS).

How Do Core Web Vitals Affect SEO?

Core Web Vitals are incorporated into Google's Page Experience ranking factors. Poor performance in these metrics can negatively impact your website's search engine ranking, while good performance can enhance it.

Can I Ignore Core Web Vitals if My Content Is Strong?

While strong content is crucial, poor Core Web Vitals can affect your site's visibility and user experience, which ultimately can lead to lower engagement and conversions. So, it's best not to ignore them.

What Tools Can I Use to Measure Core Web Vitals?

Several tools like Google's Web Vitals Extension, Lighthouse, and Chrome DevTools can help you measure these metrics. Other third-party tools like WebPageTest.org and GTmetrix are also useful.

How Often Should I Check My Core Web Vitals?

It's advisable to monitor your Core Web Vitals regularly, especially after making significant changes to your website. Automated tools can help keep track of your performance over time.

Is There a Difference Between Desktop and Mobile Core Web Vitals?

Yes, Core Web Vitals can behave differently on desktop and mobile due to varying hardware and network conditions. It's important to optimise for both.

Are Core Web Vitals the Only Metrics I Should Focus On?

While Core Web Vitals are important, they're part of a larger picture of web performance and user experience. Other metrics like Time to First Byte (TTFB) and Total Blocking Time (TBT) are also valuable.

Do Core Web Vitals Apply to All Types of Websites?

Yes, regardless of the type of website you have—be it an eCommerce store, a blog, or a portfolio site—Core Web Vitals are universal metrics that apply.

What Are Some Quick Wins for Improving Core Web Vitals?

Image optimisation, lazy loading, and asynchronous loading of non-critical scripts are some quick ways to improve Core Web Vitals. Additionally, server optimisation can help with faster content delivery.

Chapter 25

Appendix

_____

Glossary

A concise dictionary of terms related to Core Web Vitals and web performance to help you understand jargon and acronyms.

- **LCP**: Largest Contentful Paint
- **FID**: First Input Delay
- **CLS**: Cumulative Layout Shift
- **TTFB**: Time to First Byte
- **TBT**: Total Blocking Time
- **PWA**: Progressive Web App

- **SEO**: Search Engine Optimisation

Further Reading

For those looking to deepen their understanding, here are some recommended books and academic papers:

1. **"High-Performance Browser Networking" by Ilya Grigorik**
2. **"Web Performance in Action" by Jeremy L. Wagner**
3. **"Building Progressive Web Apps" by Tal Ater**
4. **"JavaScript: The Good Parts" by Douglas Crockford**
5. **Academic Papers from the ACM Digital Library related to Web Performance**

Additional Resources

Online platforms, tools, and communities for continued learning and updates:

1. **Web.dev**: Comprehensive tutorials and articles on web performance.

2. **MDN Web Docs**: Extensive documentation covering all aspects of web development.
3. **Coursera & Udemy**: Platforms offering courses related to web performance.
4. **GitHub**: Various repositories are dedicated to the subject of web performance.
5. **Stack Overflow**: A community of developers where you can ask questions and share your knowledge.
6. **Reddit Subforums**: Such as r/webdev and r/frontend for staying updated on new trends and discussions.
7. **Google Webmaster Blog**: For official updates and announcements related to web performance.